D I S C O V

B E G I N N I N G   I M P R O V I S A T I O N

AN IMPROVISATION PRIMER

K E Y B O A R D   D I S C O V E R Y   L I B R A R Y

By Nancy & Randall Faber
with Edwin McLean

Production: Frank and Gail Hackinson
Production Coordinator: Marilyn Cole
Cover and Illustrations: Terpstra Design, San Francisco
Engraving: Fallström Ltd., Hollywood, Florida

FABER
PIANO ADVENTURES®
3042 Creek Drive
Ann Arbor, Michigan 48108

Note to Teachers

The ability to improvise can be developed rather easily. **Discover Beginning Improvisation** is designed for students of all ages who have had no previous experience improvising. This book lays a foundation for creativity and self-expression using the simplest possible exercises in imaginative settings.

The exercises in the *Discover Improvisation* series are foolproof. They inspire the student to be creative, while being great fun for both student and teacher.

Discover Beginning Improvisation is the first book in the *Discover Improvisation* series. This improvisation primer gently launches the student into the exploration of sounds. It helps the student to discover the expressive possibilities of dynamics, articulation, as well as consonance and dissonance.

The Keyboard Discovery Library fosters "discovery learning"—learning through exploration and discovery. Each series in the library provides creative structures which allow the student to experiment and explore.

Helpful Hints

1. Any of the exercises can be used as duets or ensemble pieces by transposing the left hand parts up an octave or two and embellishing the rhythm.

2. A drum machine or computer can be an effective "extra musician." If drum sounds are used, the left hand should be practiced alone with drums before adding the right hand part.

3. Right and left hand coordination may be difficult at first for beginning students. If so, the teacher should play the left hand parts so that the student can concentrate on the creative aspects of the exercise. (In addition, the left hand and/or accompaniments may be recorded during the lesson for home practice by the student.)

Using the Audio

 A track number is displayed in a triangle with each musical example to help coordinate book and online audio. At the beginning of each track there will be one measure of drums to set the tempo.

 Visit **pianoadventures.com/dbimprov** to access online audio, MP3 downloads and MIDI files.

GENERAL MIDI Online downloads include standard MIDI files for use with your computer, keyboard, or synthesizer. Download the files to your computer to access or to save the MIDI files to your hard drive, floppy disk, or USB Flash drive.

ISBN 978-1-61677-051-8

ontents

Exploring the Black Keys

Exploring Listening

Exploring Half Steps

Exploring Whole Steps

Exploring the Major 5-finger Scale

Exploring the Minor 5-finger Scale

Exploring the C Major Scale

▶ The Old Cowboy

How to Play . . .

The old cowboy has only one good hand for riding his horse.
You will be making up or *improvising* a tune for him with your right hand, while your teacher plays along with you.

1. Create your own melody.
Use the 5 black keys given above, in any order.

Set your right hand over the keys and let your teacher begin.
Get the feel of the beat *before* you begin playing.

2. To end "The Old Cowboy," play softer and softer as the cowboy rides away into the sunset.

Teacher Accompaniment
With an easy swing (not fast)

What the Old Cowboy is Thinking

The old cowboy only knows 5 notes.

This 5-note scale is called a **pentatonic scale**.

Penta means five. **Tonic** means tone. **Pentatonic** = 5 tones.

"Writing" the Range

On the keyboard below, color in the notes of the pentatonic scale used in "The Old Cowboy."

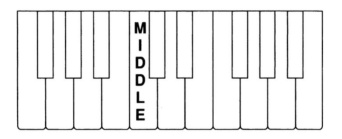

Name each note below.

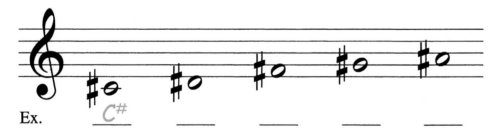

Ex. $C^{\#}$

Circle the correct answer.

1. **Penta** means
   - a. five
   - b. six
   - c. one

2. **Tonic** means
   - a. time
   - b. tone
   - c. tricky

3. **Pentatonic** means
   - a. time to go home
   - b. an apartment
   - c. 5 tones

4. **Improvise** means
   - a. herd cattle
   - b. time to go home
   - c. create "on the spot"
   - d. practice with the metronome

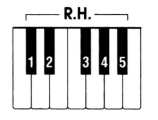

▶ **2** # Sounds from the East

R.H.

L.H.

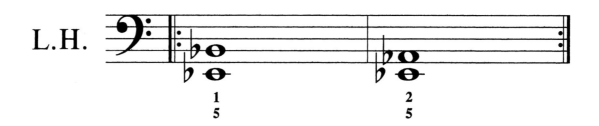

1
5

2
5

How to Play . . .

You will be using the same 5 black keys as in "The Old Cowboy."
This time the notes have been spelled as *flats*. Set your R.H. over these keys.

L.H.　Begin by playing 4 measures of left hand alone. This will help you set a steady beat.
(Notice that the left hand keeps repeating, back and forth.)

R.H.　Bring in the right hand, using the 5 black keys in any order.
When you feel ready, move around to any other black keys on the piano.

Optional accompanying keyboard parts: (for 2 pianos or for keyboard sequencing)

Accomp. 1

Accomp. 2

FF10

Ancient Oriental Writings

"Sounds from the East" also uses the **pentatonic scale.**
This time the notes are spelled with flats.

Name each note below.

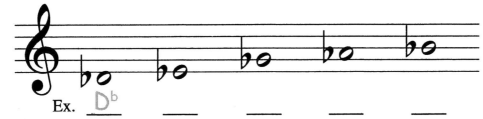

Ex. $\underline{D^b}$ ___ ___ ___ ___

Pagoda

The first line of music in "Pagoda" has already been written for you.
Write in your own right hand for the second line of music.

You may want to improvise many possible endings.
An improvisation that is written down becomes a musical **composition**.

mf

(Remember, on the staff the flat is written **before** the note.)

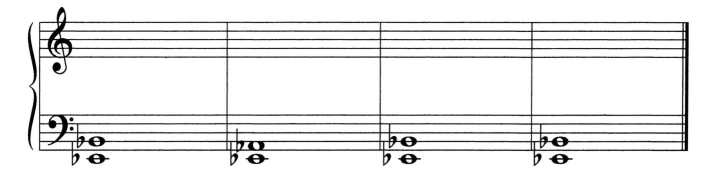

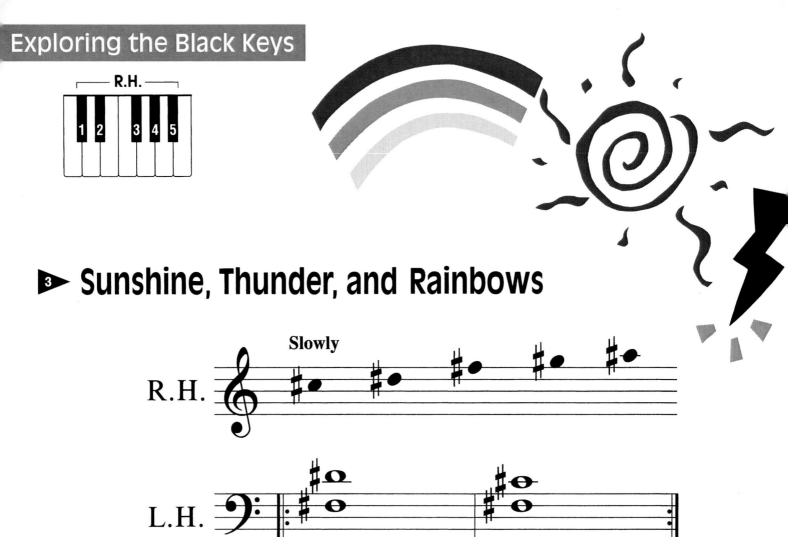

▶ Sunshine, Thunder, and Rainbows

How to Play . . .

You will be using the same 5 black keys as in "Sounds from the East," only played **1 octave higher**. This time the notes have been spelled as **sharps.**

1. **Sunshine**

   L.H.   Begin "Sunshine" by playing 4 measures of *L.H. alone.*
   R.H.   Improvise using the 5 notes given above, in any order.

2. **Thunder**

   When you are ready, make the storm arrive!
   Press down the right foot pedal.
   Using either white or black keys:

   • play *high sounds* to make *lightning.*
   • play *low sounds* to make *thunder.*

   Keep holding the pedal down. The storm can last as long as you wish!

3. **Rainbow**

   While still holding the pedal down, end the storm with a rainbow:
   L.H.   Use the same left hand as in "Sunshine."
   R.H.   Use the same 5 black keys, but this time an *octave higher.*

   End with a calm, peaceful sound.

Weather Report

Our weather report for Pentatonic City shows that the temperature will be rising sharply five degrees.

The temperature has been mapped below using musical notes!

Name each note below.

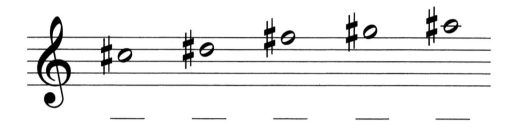

Can you make the temperature fall 5 degrees?
(Draw in the notes.)

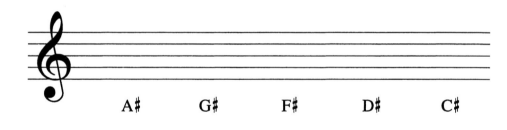

A♯　　　G♯　　　F♯　　　D♯　　　C♯

On the Spot Weather Coverage

Using your R.H. on just the black keys, create music for these weather conditions:
(Use the pedal if you wish.)

- A cloud passing dreamily overhead

- The sun beating down at 98 degrees

- Big, soft snowflakes falling softly

- Hail stones sending people running for cover.

Play any of the above ideas for your family or friends, and see if they can guess which weather condition you chose!

If they guess incorrectly, give them another chance.

Have fun creating the weather!

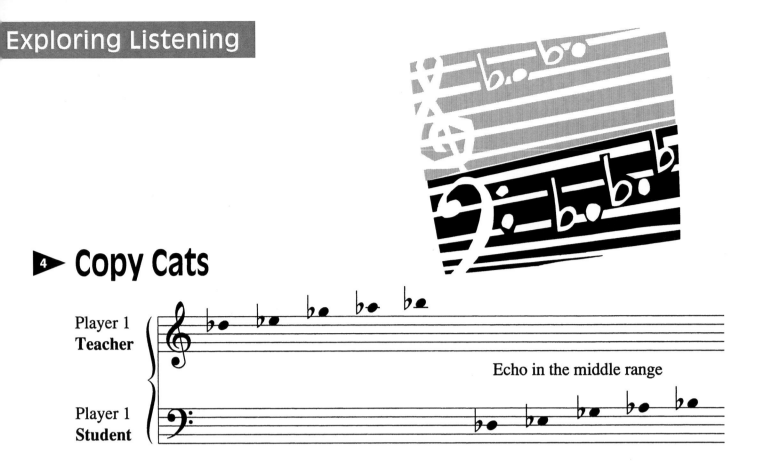

▶ Copy Cats

Being able to imitate or copy sounds is a useful skill in improvising.
"Copy Cats" will help you learn to imitate rhythms.

Preparatory Drill:

Clap each rhythm twice with your teacher.
Do not pause between rhythms A, B, and C.

How to Play . . .

Set your hand over the keys for **"Copy Cats."** Set a steady beat by tapping
(or turning on a metronome or drum machine).

1. The teacher begins by improvising a short melody using rhythm A, B, or C.
   Listen carefully.

2. You must immediately echo back *the same rhythm,* without missing a beat.
   You may use *any* of the above black keys for your echo!

3. Your teacher then continues with a new rhythm, and you again answer the same way.
   Continue this copy cat improvisation over and over!

The goal is never to miss a beat between teacher and student.

Don't stop to correct mistakes!

The Copy Machine

Copy each musical example onto the staff on the right.
Try to make your "copy" look as neat as the original. Then name each note.

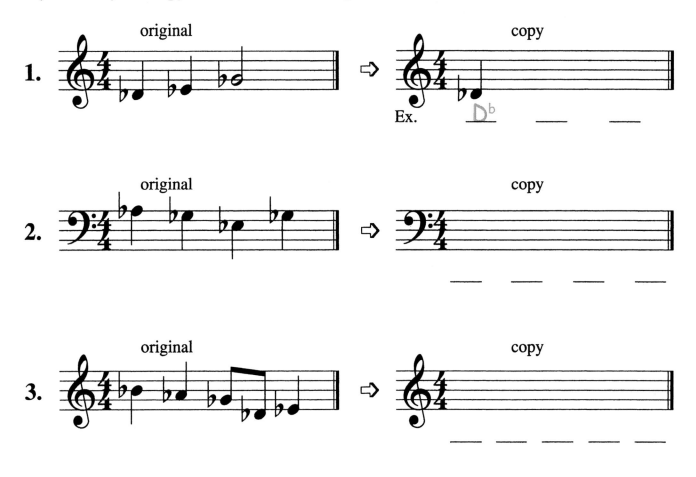

LISTEN UP!

Your teacher will play example 1, 2, 3, or 4 above. Circle which one is played.

Super Copy Cat:

This week improvise **"Copy Cats"** on your own.

1. Have your **right hand** play the teacher part (Player 1).

2. Have your **left hand** (Player 2) copy it.

Half Steps:

From one key to the very next key is a **half step**.

Find and **play** these half steps on the piano.

Say aloud "half step" as you play.

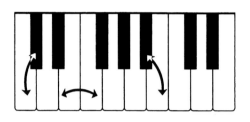

In the improvisations below, you will use only **half steps!**

Half-Step Rhythms

Play the rhythms below using half steps on the piano.

Choose a half step that you think best fits the words and pictures to the right.

Would it be | HIGH or LOW? | | LOUD or SOFT? | | FAST or SLOW? |

Remember, it must only be a half step!

1. a giant walking

2. a cricket chirping

chirp

3. a faraway drum

4. two bees talking

Bzzz

▶ The Haunted Castle

You are standing outside the door of a mysterious haunted castle.
If you knock the correct number of times, a giant will let you in!

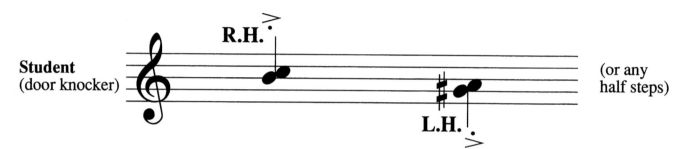

Student
(door knocker)

(or any
half steps)

How to Play . . .

1. First listen to the slow weird music coming from inside the castle (your teacher's part). Choose a number between 1 and 8, then try knocking 1 to 8 times, using the notes above. Knock in rhythm to the weird music.

2. If you have knocked the correct number of times, the giant (your teacher) will play 4 magic chords and then let you in. If not, try another number. (Teacher: see instructions below.)

3. Once you are inside the castle, play a creepy chord using all of the notes given above (or any combination of half steps).

Teacher (giant) Part

1. Select a number between 1 and 8, but don't tell the student. Begin playing **Part A**.

2. When the student has knocked the correct number of times, play **Part B**.

(Optional: While you are playing Part A, make vocal sounds characteristic of a haunted castle: "Ooooh, wooooh, ooooh…" etc.)

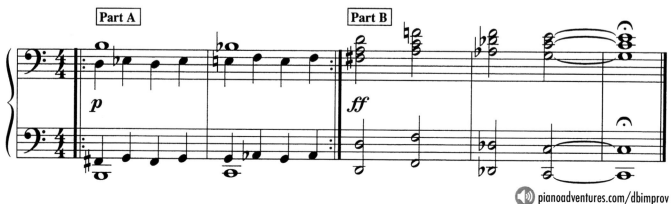

pianoadventures.com/dbimprov

Preparatory Drill:

Practicing this drill will help you get the feel of the "Magic Carpet Ride."

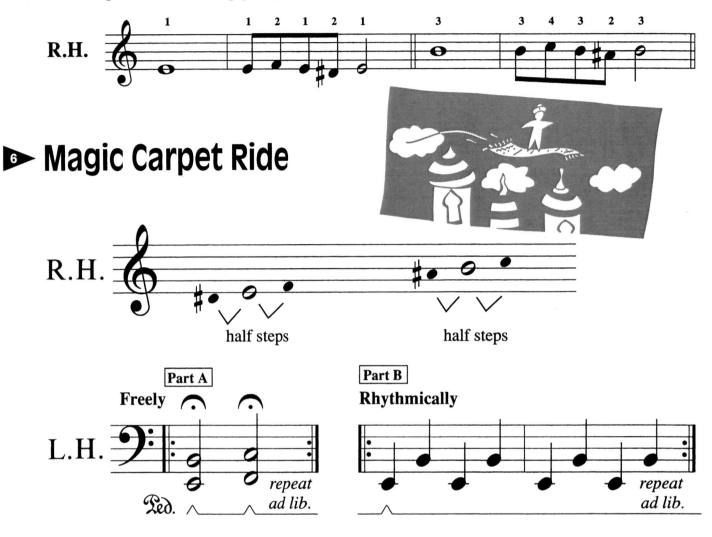

▶ Magic Carpet Ride

half steps   half steps

Part A
Freely

Part B
Rhythmically

repeat
ad lib.

repeat
ad lib.

How to Play . . .

1. *Warm up the magic carpet* by freely improvising the R.H. over the L.H. 5ths.
   R.H. Use E and B—and the notes a half step *above* and *below* them, as shown.
   L.H. Hold each L.H. chord as long as you wish, using pedal.

2. *The magic carpet starts moving.*
   L.H. Begin with the L.H. alone, using the part B pattern shown above.
   R.H. When the magic carpet is moving very steadily, play R.H. notes high on the keyboard. (Choose from the same notes as before.) Keep the rhythm simple, using mostly whole notes.

3. *Land the magic carpet* by repeating Part A (number 1 above).

Creative Hints . . .

• Try using E's and B's from many different octaves.
• Try adding other white keys as filler notes.

Whole Steps:

A **whole** step is made up of 2 half steps.
On the keyboard, a whole step is **2 keys** with one key in-between.

Find and play these whole steps on the piano.

Say aloud "whole step" as you play.

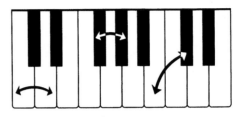

A Whole Lot of Whole Steps!

Put a check (✓) on the key a **whole step higher** than the keys marked X.

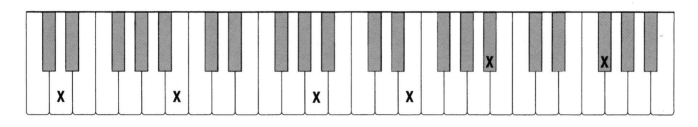

Put a check (✓) on the key a **whole step lower** than the keys marked X.

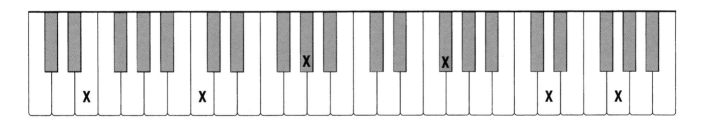

On the keyboards below, build scales which use only whole steps.
Continue up by whole steps from the notes given, marking each key with an X.

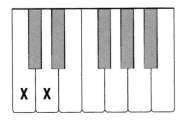   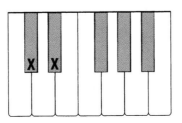

Find and play these notes on the piano. Try them with the pedal depressed.

► Car Honks

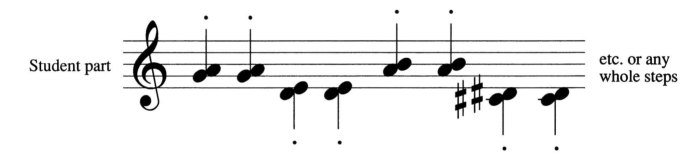

Student part

etc. or any
whole steps

How to Play . . .

1. Tell your teacher (the car engine) when to start.

2. Make up honking rhythms using the 2nds above or any whole steps.

   Hint: The 2nds may be repeated several times before changing.

3. Tell the car engine (your teacher) when to **slow down** and when to **speed up**.
   Watch out! Your car (teacher) may stop suddenly. If so, you are in a traffic jam.
   Honking your horn will start you moving again.

Teacher part (car engine)

Fast and lively or as directed by student, with occasional sudden stops.

repeat
ad lib.

FF10

► The Martian and the Earthling
AN OUTERSPACE JAM SESSION

A Martian and an earthling are making music together using only whole steps.

Your right hand will be the Martian, and your left hand will be the earthling!

How to Play . . .

Hold the pedal down throughout.

L.H. (earthling) — Begin with 4 measures of the left hand alone.
(Repeat the 4 notes shown above, over and over.)

R.H. (Martian) — Improvise outer space melodies, using the 5 notes shown above.

Creative hint: When you are ready, try jumping to different octaves with your right hand playing loud or soft.
You can also play two notes at the same time with your right hand.

To end your "jam session," play the R.H. whole step pattern on the highest keys of the piano!

▶ Musette in C

A **musette** is a dance in $\frac{4}{4}$ time that imitates a bagpipe.

In this improvisation, the L.H. is the bagpipe.
Notice the R.H. uses only 5 white keys —C D E F G.

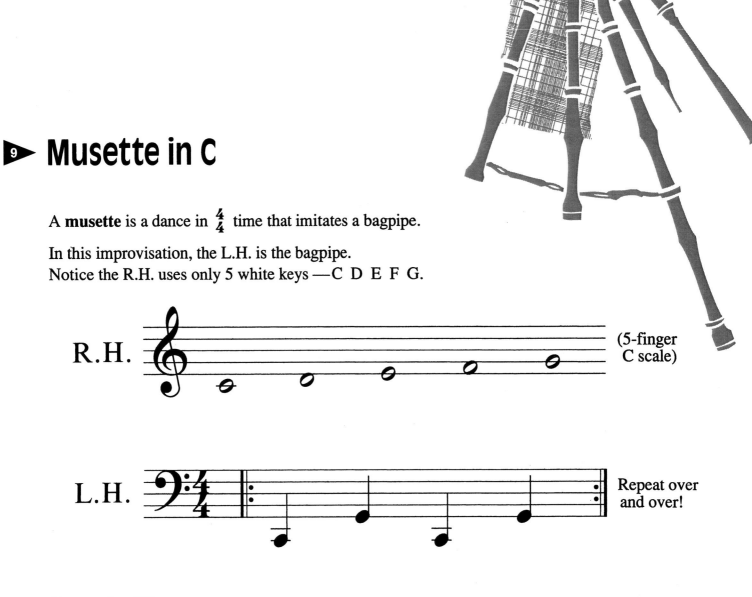

R.H.   (5-finger C scale)

L.H.   Repeat over and over!

How to Play . . .

L.H.   Set a steady beat by beginning with 2 measures of the left hand alone.

R.H.   Create a *simple* melody choosing from the notes C, D, E, F, or G.

End your musette on C with both hands.

Teacher Tip: Stylistically, this musette could be reminiscent of Bach's *Musette in D*, only slower. It is shown here transposed.

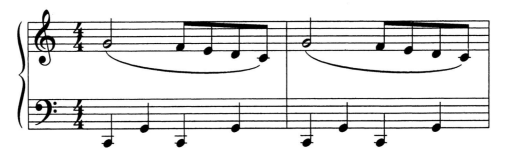

Learning the Major 5-Finger Scale

1. Mark the whole steps (W) and half steps (H) for the 5 notes below.

Ex.   W   ___   ___   ___

This is called the **C major 5-finger scale.**

2. Find this **W-W-H-W** pattern on G, and on D.

Say aloud "Start: **Whole - Whole - Half - Whole.**"

3. Try improvising musettes using G and D positions.

Billy the Bagpiper

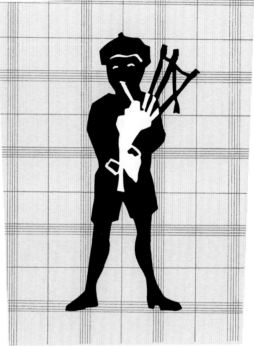

Compose a piece below for Billy. The left hand is already written.

Write your melody, choosing from the notes C D E F G.
Use the rhythm given above each measure.

REVIEW:

The **major** 5-finger scale is "Whole-Whole-Half-Whole."

NEW:

For a darker, scary, or sad sound, use a **minor** 5-finger scale.

Play the D minor 5-finger scale shown below, saying

"**Whole-<u>Half</u>-Whole-Whole**"

Notice the half step is between notes **2 and 3**.

◄ The Sad Beast

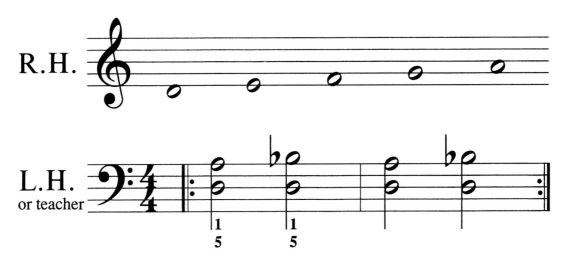

How to Play . . .

The "Sad Beast" uses the minor 5-finger scale.

L.H.   Start the Sad Beast walking with 2 measures of L.H. alone. Set a slow steady beat.

R.H.   Bring in the R.H., using the 5 notes given above in any order. Keep it simple.

For variety, try playing in different octaves with either hand.

End the improvisation with both hands playing a D.

Major 5-finger scale

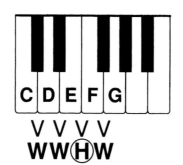

C D E F G

V V V V

WW(H)W

Minor 5-finger scale

D E F G A

V V V V

W(H)WW

Notice where the half steps are!

Nothing is Finer than Major and Minor!

1. Mark the whole steps and half steps for each position below. Circle major or minor.

2. Then improvise a short melody based on the idea shown to the right.

Should it be | HIGH or LOW? | | LOUD or SOFT? | | FAST or SLOW? |

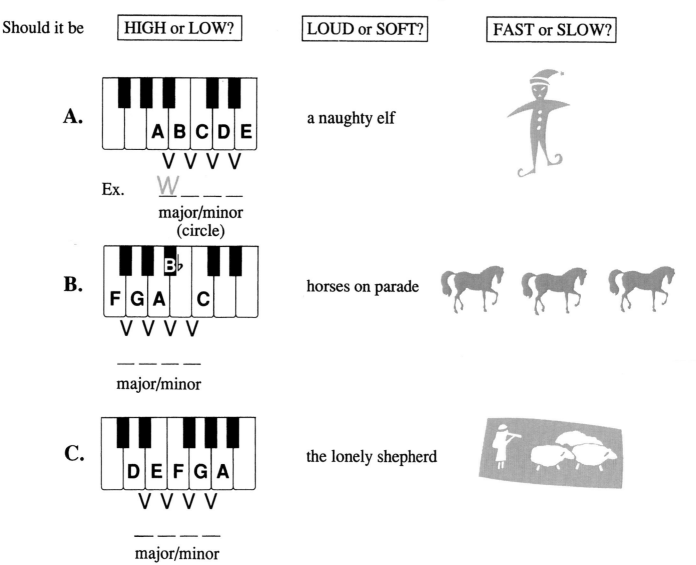

A.

A B C D E

V V V V

Ex. W __ __ __

major/minor
(circle)

a naughty elf

B.

B♭

F G A C

V V V V

__ __ __ __

major/minor

horses on parade

C.

D E F G A

V V V V

__ __ __ __

major/minor

the lonely shepherd

⏩ A Song of Peace

This improvisation uses the complete **C major scale.**

Preparatory Drill:

Practice the C major scale with the R.H. until you can easily play it *going up* and *going down.*

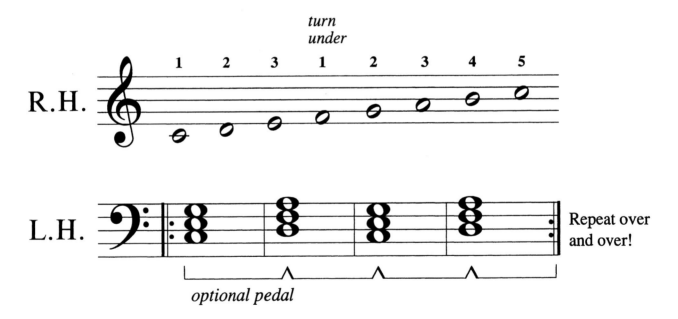

optional pedal

How to Play . . .

L.H. Play 4 measures of left hand alone for an introduction.
You may also use the damper pedal (right foot pedal).

R.H. Bring in the right hand using notes from the C major scale.
Use mostly *steps.*

Begin and end your improvisation *softly.*

More About the C Major Scale

Mark whole and half steps on the C major scale below.

(Use **W** for whole and **H** for half.)

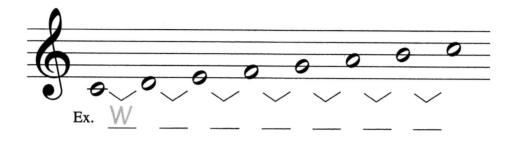

Ex. W

The Tool Box
FOR IMPROVISERS

Draw a line connecting each example to the correct tool in the box.

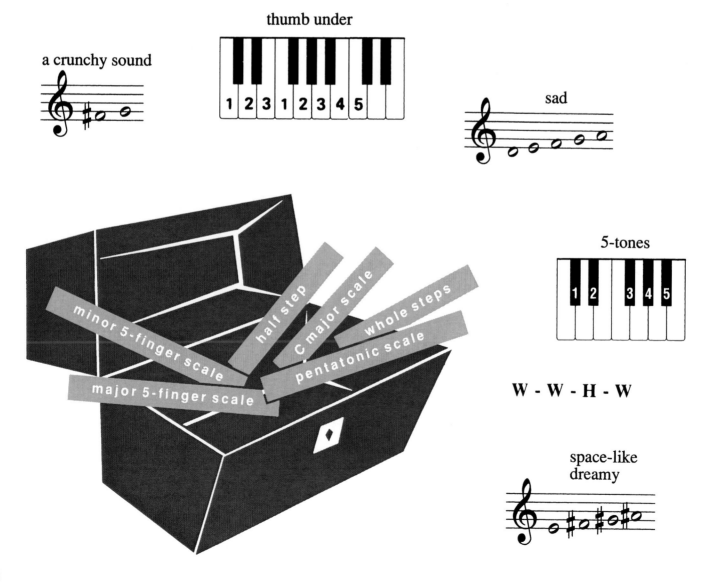

a crunchy sound

thumb under

sad

5-tones

W - W - H - W

space-like
dreamy

Certificate
of
Completion

Congratulations! You have completed Discover Beginning Improvisation!

Name: _____

Date: _____

Teacher: _____

You are now ready for:

Discover Blues Improvisation

(Discover Improvisation, Book 1)